PRAYER AND STUDY GUIDE

THE POWER OF A *Praying*® Husband

STORMIE OMARTIAN

HARVEST HOUSE PUBLISHERS
Eugene, Oregon 97402

Cover by Koechel Peterson & Associates, Minneapolis, Minnesota

THE POWER OF A PRAYING® HUSBAND PRAYER AND STUDY GUIDE
Copyright © 2002 by Stormie Omartian
Published by Harvest House Publishers
Eugene, Oregon 97402

Library of Congress Cataloging-in-Publication Data
ISBN 0-7369-0850-1

Printed in the United States of America

02 03 04 05 06 07 08 09 / BC-CF/ 10 9 8 7 6 5 4 3 2 1

THIS BOOK IS THE PROPERTY OF

_____

Please do not read beyond this page without
permission of the person named above.

CONTENTS

How to Get Started

You are to be commended for taking seriously your role as spiritual leader in your family. As you pray for your wife in depth, you will be rewarded in many ways, and your marriage will be greatly enriched.

All You Will Need

This prayer and study guide is designed to help you determine how to pray more specifically for yourself, your wife, and your marriage. It is divided into a 20-week plan for use in personal or group study. You will need to have the book *The Power of a Praying Husband* and a Bible that you are not hesitant to write in. The New King James Version is used in this book, but other versions will also work.

Time to Get Personal

Some of the questions in this study are very personal, so keep this book in a private place. Your answers are not for others to read, but rather to help you think clearly about each area of prayer focus as it relates to your own circumstances. The questions will assist you in determining specifically what you and your wife's prayer needs are, and will help you know how to pray. Don't think in terms of giving right or wrong answers, just be concerned with the honest truth so you can have clarity and direction. Try to write an answer for each question or direction, even if it is only one sentence or a few words. And don't underestimate the power of writing out a prayer when this is suggested. These prayers can be as long or as short as you want to make them.

WORKING ALONE

Once you have read "The Power" and chapter one, "Her Husband," and have answered the questions for Week One, you can proceed in any order if there are pressing issues you want to pray about right away.

IN A GROUP

In a group study of two or more men, it's best to follow the order in this book so that the group will be on the same page when it comes together each week. After you have read the appropriate chapter in *The Power of a Praying Husband* and have answered the questions in this prayer and study guide on your own, the leader will bring the group together and go over each question to see what insight God has given you. Though you may not want to share personal information in the group, feel free to share what God has spoken to your heart or what His Word has revealed to you. It will be a great encouragement to the others.

WEEK ONE

*Read "The Power" and chapter one, "Her Husband,"
from The Power of a Praying Husband*

These two sections of the book are the longest because they
are the most crucial to the success of your prayers. After
you have read them, take each of these questions before
the Lord and ask Him to show you the truth. Your honest
answers will pave the way for life-changing intercession.

1. Read Proverbs 18:22 and underline it in your Bible. In
   light of that scripture, complete the following sentence:
   "God has given me favor because I have _____ ."
   Do you sense God's favor in that respect? _____
   What blessings have you enjoyed because you are mar-
   ried to your wife?

2. Read Matthew 19:5 and underline it in your Bible. In light of that scripture, complete the following sentence: "I am joined with my wife and we have become _____." Do you believe that you and your wife are truly one? _____ Do you believe that your wife has a strong sense that the two of you are one? _____ Write a prayer below asking God to give you and your wife a greater sense of what it means to be one with each other.

3. Read John 15:13 and underline it in your Bible. In light of that scripture, what is the greatest act of love you can show toward your wife? _____ What is a good way to lay down your life for your wife without physically dying? _____ (See "How to Really Love Your Wife" on page 26 in *The Power of a Praying Husband*.) Write a prayer asking God to help you to lay down your life for your wife in prayer.

4. Read Luke 10:19 and underline it in your Bible. According to this scripture, God gives you authority over all the power of _____. Do you believe you have authority over the enemy in your wife's life? _____ Is there any area where you see that the enemy is trying to (or already has tried to) hurt your wife or drive a wedge between you and your wife? _____ Explain your answer.

5. Read 1 Peter 3:7 and underline it in your Bible. According to this scripture, what could hinder your prayers?

_____

_____

_____

Have you ever behaved toward your wife in a manner that might hinder your prayers? _____ Explain your answer and write a prayer asking God to keep you from doing anything that might prevent your prayers from being answered.

6. Read Ephesians 5:25 and underline it in your Bible. How are you supposed to love your wife? _____

   _____

   In what ways does Christ love you that are good examples of how you should love your wife?

7. Read 1 Peter 3:8 and underline it in your Bible. Are there any areas in your marriage where you believe you and your wife are not of one mind? _____ Explain your answer and write out a prayer asking God to bring you and your wife into greater unity than you have ever been before.

8. The power in your prayers is _____. Your prayers
   for your wife enable her to better _____
   _____ and respond to _____.
   (See page 23, last paragraph, in *The Power of a Praying
   Husband*.) Do you find it easy or difficult to make a commitment to pray regularly for your wife?_____
   _____ Explain. Write a prayer asking
   God to help you pray powerfully for your wife on a con-
   sistent basis.

9. Do you consider yourself to be compassionate toward
   your wife? _____ Does your wife consider you to be
   compassionate toward her? _____ (Ask her if you don't
   know the answer.) In light of your answers, write a
   prayer asking God to give you a *greater* heart of com-
   passion for your wife than you have ever had before.

10. Describe the love you have for your wife. Do you believe your wife understands the full extent of how you feel about her?

11. List some of the things you do that show love for your wife. Do you think she clearly perceives those things you do as love for her?

12. What are some new ways you could show love for your
wife that you know she would appreciate? _____

_____

_____

Write out a prayer asking God to help you show uncon-
ditional love toward your wife in ways she can clearly
perceive.

13. Are you holding on to any unforgiveness toward your
wife? _____ If you answered yes, explain why and
then write out a prayer confessing it to God and asking
Him to help you forgive her completely. If you
answered no, write out a prayer asking God to keep you
free from any hidden resentment or unforgiveness
toward your wife.

14. Is there anything your wife does that irritates or bothers you? _____ If you answered yes, explain your answer and write a prayer about it. If your answer is no, write a prayer thanking God for your wife.

15. Read Psalm 62:5 and underline it in your Bible. In light of this scripture, in whom should you put your expectations? _____ Do you have any expectations of your wife that she fails to meet? _____ Do you believe she has any expectations of you that you fail to meet? _____ Write a prayer asking God to help you and your wife put your expectations in Him and not entirely in each other.

16. If there is one thing you could change about your wife, what would it be? Write out a prayer asking God to either make that change in her or change your expectations.

17. Do you ever talk to your wife in a way that is less than courteous, respectful, or pleasing in God's sight? _____ If you answered yes, write a prayer below confessing that and asking God to give you words and actions that bless your wife. If you answered no, pat yourself on the back and then write out a prayer asking God to help you continue to speak words that bring life, love, and edification to your wife and family.

18. Is there anything about you that you know irritates or bothers your wife? _____ If you answered yes, tell what it is and how you could pray about it. (If you are not sure, ask your wife.) If you answered no, tell how you learned to be such a wonderful husband.

19. Read Luke 18:1 and James 5:16 and underline them in your Bible. What do these verses speak to you as a praying husband?

20. Pray the prayer on page 44 of *The Power of a Praying Husband* out loud. Include your own specific needs.

Read chapter two, "Her Spirit,"
from *The Power of a Praying Husband*

1. In light of page 47 of *The Power of a Praying Husband*, to
    what kind of automobile would you compare your wife?
    Be specific and explain your answer.

2. Do you ever see signs in your wife that she is running on
    empty? _____ If you answered yes, what are those
    signs? If you answered no, is that because your wife
    never gets depleted, or because you don't see the signs?
    Explain.

3. Do you believe your wife desires to be a strong woman of God? _____ In accordance with your answer, write a prayer asking God to help your wife become the woman He created her to be.

4. When it comes to her spiritual growth and relationship with God, what do you think your wife needs most (for example, time in the Word, discipline to pray, and so on)? If you don't know, ask your wife and write down what she says.

5. Read Matthew 5:6 and underline it in your Bible. What is the reward for someone who hungers and thirsts after God's way of life? _____ Write out a prayer for your wife that she will hunger and thirst for the righteousness of God.

6. Read John 15:7 and underline it in your Bible. If your wife walks closely with God and His Word lives in her, what will be her reward?

7. Read Romans 10:17 and underline it in your Bible. In light of that scripture, what is one way you could pray for your wife to increase her faith?

8. How could your marriage be positively affected by your wife having a stronger relationship with God?

9. Read Matthew 17:20 and underline it in your Bible. Does your wife have faith strong enough to believe that with God nothing is impossible? _____ Write a prayer asking God to continually increase your wife's faith so that she always believes that.

10. Pray the prayer on pages 51–52 of *The Power of a Praying Husband* out loud. Include specifics about your wife's relationship with God.

WEEK THREE

Read chapter three, "Her Emotions,"
from *The Power of a Praying Husband*

1. Does your wife ever experience negative or upsetting emotions?_____ If you answered yes, write a short prayer asking God to show you both the root cause of these negative emotions. If you answered no, write a short prayer asking God to keep your wife in perfect peace.

2. Ask your wife if there is any negative emotion she is currently experiencing, or has experienced in the recent past. Then ask her how she would like you to pray for her regarding that. Record her answer below.

3. Does what your wife experiences in her emotions ever affect you or other members of your family?_____ Explain your answer. Describe how your wife's emotions affect you or your children.

4. How do you generally react to your wife's emotions? Do you ever have trouble understanding them? Explain your answer.

5. Write a short prayer asking God to help you react to your wife's emotions in a way that supports her and helps her find peace.

6. Read Romans 8:6 and underline it in your Bible. Write out this scripture as a prayer for your wife. For example, "Lord, I pray that (<u>wife's name</u>) will not be carnally minded, which is death, but will be..." and so on.

7. Read Romans 12:10-12 and underline it in your Bible. Write it out below as a prayer for your wife. For example, "Lord, I pray that (<u>wife's name</u>) will be kind and affectionate to others..." and so on.

8. Is there anything that you ever do or say, or *don't* do or say, that triggers certain negative emotions in your wife? _____ If you answered yes, explain how you could pray for yourself about that. If you answered no, ask your wife about that—just to make sure—and record what she says below.

9. Read Proverbs 12:25 and underline it in your Bible. In light of that scripture, what could you do to help keep anxiety or depression from overcoming your wife? (Ask God to show you specifics.)

10. Pray the prayer on pages 61–62 of *The Power of a Praying Husband* out loud. Include specifics about your wife's emotions.

WEEK FOUR

Read chapter four, "Her Motherhood,"
from *The Power of a Praying Husband*

1. Is your wife at peace with being a mother or not being a mother? _____ What is her greatest concern or struggle with being a mother or not being a mother? (Don't assume anything. Ask her if you are not absolutely sure.) This is an extremely important question. Many problems can be prevented by knowing the full answer to it and praying accordingly.

2. Do you feel that your wife has achieved a successful balance between being a good wife and a good mother? _____ Do you ever feel that your wife cares more about being a good mother than she does being a good wife? Explain.

3. What would your wife say is the most difficult thing she has to face in regard to being a mother, or *not* being a mother? (Ask her if you are not sure.) Explain. Write out a prayer for her about that.

4. Does your wife ever feel guilty, or feel as if she has failed in some way as a mother? _____ Explain your answer and write out a prayer for her about that.

5. Do you ever feel guilty in regard to being a father? _____ Explain your answer and write out a prayer asking God to make you the father He wants you to be.

6. What is one way you can be more involved in your children's lives, especially when you have to be away from them? (See page 69, first paragraph, in *The Power of a Praying Husband*.) _____
_____ Write a prayer asking God to make you a powerful praying father.

7. Read Proverbs 31:28 and underline it in your Bible. Does this accurately sum up the way things are at your house? _____ Explain your answer. Write out a prayer for your family using this scripture. For example, "Lord, I pray that our children will rise up and…" and so on.

8. Read Isaiah 65:23 and underline it in your Bible. Write it out below as a declaration for your family. For example, "In the name of Jesus, I say that my wife and I will not labor in vain, nor…" and so on.

9. Do you feel that your wife has a good relationship with each of her children? _____ Do you feel that *you* have a good relationship with each of your children? _____ Write out a prayer naming each child and ask God to bless their relationship with their mother and with you.

10. Pray the prayer on pages 73–74 of *The Power of a Praying Husband* out loud. Include specifics about your wife as a mother.

WEEK FIVE

Read chapter five, "Her Moods,"
from *The Power of a Praying Husband*

1. Does your wife ever have what seems to you to be a sudden mood swing? _____ Explain your answer.

2. Do you feel that the balance of hormones or degree of health in your wife's body is sometimes reflected in her moods or attitudes? _____ Explain and describe how you could pray about that.

3. What is usually your first reaction to your wife's mood swing or attitude change?

4. Do you feel that your reaction to your wife's mood changes could benefit from prayer? _____ How could you pray about that?

5. Read Philippians 4:6,7 and underline it in your Bible. In light of that scripture, what will guard your wife's heart and mind? _____ Write out this scripture as a prayer for your wife. For example, "Lord, I pray that (wife's name) will be anxious for nothing, but in everything..." and so on.

6. Read Psalm 119:165 and underline it in your Bible. In light of that scripture, what would give your wife peace? _____ Write this scripture as a prayer for your wife. For example, "Lord, I pray that (<u>wife's name</u>) will love Your law and have..." and so on.

7. Of the ten things you could say to your wife on pages 79–80 of *The Power of a Praying Husband*, what is the one your wife would most love to hear from you? Why?

8. When your wife has mood swings, what does she say is the reason for them? _____ _____ Does she hold you responsible for any part of it? _____ Explain. How could you pray about that?

9. Read 2 Corinthians 10:4,5 and underline it in your Bible. Write out verse 5 as a prayer for your wife. For example, "Lord, help my wife to cast down arguments..." and so on.

10. Pray the prayer on page 83 in *The Power of a Praying Husband* out loud. Include specifics about your wife's moods.

WEEK SIX

Read chapter six, "Her Marriage,"
from *The Power of a Praying Husband*

1. Have you or your wife, or her parents or your parents,
   ever been divorced? _____ If you answered yes, write a
   prayer that asks God to break any tendency toward
   divorce in your lives. If you answered no, write a prayer
   asking God to keep divorce far from your marriage.

2. Read 1 Corinthians 7:10,11 and underline it in your
   Bible. Have you or your wife ever viewed divorce as an
   option which you would seriously consider? _____
   Explain your answer and write a prayer to break any
   thoughts of divorce you or your wife have had or might
   have in the future.

3. Do you ever sense there is anyone or any influence threatening the stability of your marriage? _____ If you answered yes, write a statement declaring to the enemy that you refuse to allow anything or anyone to destroy your marriage. Be specific. If you answered no, write a declaration to God that you will partner with Him to do whatever it takes to see that your marriage become all that He wants it to be.

4. What is your greatest concern about your marriage? (For example, "I am concerned that we could grow apart.") Write out your concern as a prayer to the Lord.

5. According to page 86 of *The Power of a Praying Husband* (first paragraph under "Seeds of Love"), what are some of the things that will grow in your wife when you plant seeds of love? _____ _____ What are some specific things you could do to make your wife feel loved or to inspire in her deeper feelings of love for you?

6. Read 1 Corinthians 10:12,13 and underline it in your Bible. In light of verse 12, what should you never assume? _____ Have you ever been tempted to commit adultery or been drawn to acts of infidelity in this marriage or in any previous marriage? _____ If you answered yes, write a prayer of repentance asking God to deliver you from all the bondages of that sin. If you answered no, write a prayer asking God to keep you from ever falling into that kind of temptation.

7. Read 1 Corinthians 10:24 and underline it in your Bible. Write out some ways in which you could seek your wife's well-being and then write a short prayer asking God to help you do those things.

8. Do either you or your wife ever speak words to each other that produce a negative response? _____ Does your wife ever feel that you don't listen to her? _____ Do you ever feel that your wife doesn't understand you? _____ In light of your answers, write a short prayer asking God to help you and your wife always communicate clearly and respectfully with one another.

9. Read Proverbs 20:3 and underline it in your Bible. Can you think of any area in your marriage where there is strife? _____ If you answered yes, write a prayer telling God about it and asking Him to help you and your wife put an end to strife. If you answered no, write a prayer asking God to help you and your wife keep strife far from your marriage relationship.

10. Pray the prayer on pages 94–95 in *The Power of a Praying Husband* aloud. Include the specifics of your marriage.

WEEK SEVEN

Read chapter seven, "Her Submission,"
from *The Power of a Praying Husband*

1. Is your wife's submission to you ever an issue in your marriage? _____ Do you feel that your wife isn't as submitted to you as you would like her to be? _____ Explain your answers.

2. Do you feel that you are completely submitted to God? _____ Does your wife feel that you are completely submitted to God? _____ Explain your answers.

3. Do you feel that your wife is able to trust God working in you? _____ Does your wife feel she is able to trust God working in you? _____ Explain your answers.

4. When a wife submits to her husband, she comes under his _____ and _____, and this frees her to become _____ _____ . (See page 100, second paragraph from the end, in *The Power of a Praying Husband*.)

5. Read Matthew 10:39 and underline it in your Bible. If you equate losing one's life in this verse to the act of submission, what will be the reward for doing so? _____ Do you believe your wife understands that concept? _____ Explain your answer and write out a prayer asking God to enable your wife to lose and find her life for the sake of the Lord.

6. In what ways do you feel you lay down your life for your wife or for the Lord? What do you gain in the process? Explain.

7. The Bible doesn't say that a husband is to demand that his wife obey him, but it does say that older women are to teach the younger women to be "obedient to their own husbands" (Titus 2:5). Are there one or more godly women in your wife's life who could teach this principle to her by example? _____ If you answered yes, who are these women and how could you pray about their relationship with your wife? If you answered no, write out a prayer that God would bring women into your wife's life who would model right order in the home. Also pray for the women who *are* in your wife's life to become godly influences.

8. Submission is easy for a woman whose husband loves her like Christ loves the church and who has her best interests at heart. Write out a prayer below asking God to make you the kind of husband to whom your wife will always find it easy to submit herself.

9. To be true submission, submission must spring from the heart. Write a prayer for your wife's heart to be so touched by the Holy Spirit and your love that godly submission will not be an issue for her.

10. Pray the prayer on page 103 of *The Power of a Praying Husband* out loud. Include specifics about your submission to the Lord and your wife's submission to you.

WEEK EIGHT

Read chapter eight, "Her Relationships,"
from *The Power of a Praying Husband*

1. Does your wife have godly female friends who are a strong support for her? _____ If you answered yes, write out a prayer asking God to protect and strengthen those relationships. If you answered no, write out a prayer asking God to help your wife find one or two good godly female friends who will be a strength and comfort to her.

2. Does your wife have a good relationship with all the members of her own family? _____ Is there a specific relationship that you know is a concern to her? _____ If you answered yes to the last question, write a prayer asking God to heal and restore that relationship. If you answered no, write a prayer asking God to bless your wife's relationship with each family member.

3. Does your wife have a good relationship with her in-laws? _____ Is there any in-law relationship that is a particular concern to her? _____ If you answered yes to the last question, write out a prayer covering that specific relationship. If you answered no, write out a prayer asking God to bless your wife's relationship with each member of your family.

4   Do you feel that your family members fully accept and love your wife? _____ If you answered yes, write a prayer asking God to always keep it that way. If you answered no, write a prayer asking God to open the hearts of your family members to fully accept and love your wife.

5. Have you ever complained about your wife to members of your family? _____ Regardless of your answer, what are some things you could say to your family members about your wife that will build her up in their eyes? Write out a prayer asking God to help you remember to do that.

6. Does your wife *feel* accepted and loved by your family? _____ (Ask her if you don't know the answer to that question.) In light of your answer, write out a prayer asking God to bless your wife's relationship with each of her in-laws in such a way that she will always feel loved and accepted by them. Be specific.

7. Are there two or three couples with whom both you and your wife enjoy spending time? _____ If you answered yes, write out a prayer asking God to protect each one of these relationships. If you answered no, write out a prayer asking God to bring such couples into your lives.

8. Read Matthew 5:23,24 and underline it in your Bible. Is there anyone with whom your wife needs to be reconciled? _____ Is your wife holding any unforgiveness toward someone? _____ Is she holding any unforgiveness toward you? _____ (If you don't know the answer to these questions, ask your wife.) If you answered yes to any of these questions, write a prayer asking God to free your wife from any unforgiveness and restore any relationship that has broken down. Be specific. If you answered no, write a prayer asking God to keep your wife free of unforgiveness toward anyone.

9. Read Proverbs 12:26 and underline it in your Bible. Does your wife have any friend in her life who you feel is not a good influence or who is draining her? _____ If you answered yes, write a prayer asking God to either take that relationship out of her life or to transform that person. If you answered no, write a prayer asking God to protect your wife from any person who would not be a positive influence.

10. Pray the prayer on page 111 of *The Power of a Praying Husband* out loud. Include specifics about your wife's relationships.

WEEK NINE

Read chapter nine, "Her Priorities,"
from *The Power of a Praying Husband*

1 Does your wife ever feel pressured or overwhelmed by
how much she has to do? Explain.

2. Does your wife find it easy or difficult to establish priorities in her life? Explain.

3. Is your wife organized, or do you feel she could stand to improve in that area? Explain.

4. Does your wife have exceptionally high expectations of herself? _____ In light of your answers to this and the previous three questions, write out a prayer for your wife specifically in regard to these things.

5. Read Matthew 6:33 and underline it in your Bible. In light of this scripture, what should be your wife's top priority? _____ Do you feel that your wife makes her relationship with God her top priority? _____ Write a prayer asking God to help your wife be able to always put Him first in her life.

6. Do you feel that in general your wife's priorities are in the right order? _____ Explain.

7. Do you ever feel that your wife puts you too low on her priority list? _____ If you answered yes, write a prayer asking God to help your wife make you a top priority in her life, right under her relationship with Him. If you answered no, write a prayer thanking God for a wife who has her priorities in the right order.

8. Does your wife have a tendency to put herself too low on her priority list? _____ If you answered yes, write a prayer asking God to give your wife the wisdom to take proper care of herself. If you answered no, write a prayer asking God to continue to give your wife the wisdom to make the care of herself a priority.

9. Read Psalm 127:1 and underline it in your Bible. Does your wife find putting together and taking care of a home an overwhelming task, or does she approach this task easily and confidently because she relies on the Lord to help her? Explain. Write a prayer asking God to take away the burdensomeness of making a home from your wife and to enable her to do it successfully.

10. Pray the prayer on pages 119–120 in *The Power of a Praying Husband* out loud. Include specifics about your wife's priorities.

WEEK TEN

Read chapter ten, "Her Beauty,"
from *The Power of a Praying Husband*

1. List the ten things you find most beautiful about your
   wife.

   1.

   2.

   3.

   4.

   5.

   6.

   7.

   8.

   9.

   10.

2. Do you think your wife sees in herself any or all of the beautiful qualities you have just listed? Explain.

3. Explain how often you tell your wife about the qualities you find beautiful or appealing in her. Write a prayer asking God to help you remember to tell your wife all the ways she is beautiful to you.

4. Read 1 Peter 3:3,4 and underline it in your Bible. According to that scripture, what is more important than physical beauty? _____ _____ Write a prayer asking God to give your wife the beauty of a gentle and quiet spirit.

5. Was your wife ever made to feel unattractive by anyone in her life? _____ (If you don't know, ask her and writer her answer here.) If you answered yes, write a prayer asking God to set your wife free from those painful memories. If you answered no, write a prayer thanking God that He protected your wife from the assaults of people who lack discernment and love.

6. Read Psalms 27:4 and 90:17 and underline them in your Bible. Write out a prayer asking God to enable your wife to always reflect the beauty of the Lord.

7. Does your wife ever look at the world's image of beauty and feel that she doesn't measure up? _____ If you answered yes, write a prayer asking God to help your wife turn her eyes away from the world and focus them on Him. If you answered no, write a prayer asking God to help your wife appreciate her own unique beauty and not be swayed by the world's standards.

8. Read Psalm 29:2 and underline it in your Bible. Write this scripture out as a prayer for your wife. For example: "Lord, help (<u>wife's name</u>) to give to You the glory due Your name..." and so on.

9. Read Proverbs 31:30 and underline it in your Bible. According to this scripture, what is more important than charm and beauty? _____ _____ Do you find that quality attractive in your wife? Why or why not?

10. Pray the prayer on page 128 of *The Power of a Praying Husband* out loud. Include specifics about your wife's beauty.

WEEK ELEVEN

Read chapter eleven, "Her Sexuality,"
from *The Power of a Praying Husband*

1. Read 1 Corinthians 7:4,5 and underline it in your Bible. According to this scripture, who has authority over your wife's body? _____ Who has authority over your body? _____ What is the main reason that you and your wife are not to deprive each other sexually?

2. Is there any way you would like to see your sexual relationship with your wife change? Explain. Write out a prayer asking God to make your sexual relationship all He designed it to be.

3. Do you feel that your wife makes the sexual aspect of your relationship enough of a priority? Explain. Write a prayer asking God to help you and your wife make your sexual relationship the priority it should be.

4. Does your wife feel attractive and loved? _____ (Ask her if you're not sure.) What are some of the things you do, or *could* do, to make your wife feel more attractive and loved?

5. Does your wife keep herself sexually attractive for you? _____ Do you keep yourself sexually attractive for your wife? _____ Is there anything either of you could do to improve yourself physically, emotionally, mentally, or spiritually for the other? Explain. Write out a prayer asking God to help you and your wife always stay physically attractive to one another.

6. Can you think of any time you have hurt your wife in a way that would cause her to withdraw from you physically and emotionally? _____ If you answered yes, have you asked her to forgive you? _____ Has she fully forgiven and released you?_____ (If you don't know the answer to these questions, ask your wife.) Write a prayer asking God to keep you and your wife free of anger, unforgiveness, and hurt so that your sexual relationship will be protected.

7. Is there physical affection between you and your wife outside of the times you are together sexually? Are you both equal contributors, or is one of you more affectionate than the other? Explain. How could you pray to see the level of affection between you improve?

8. Read 1 Thessalonians 4:3-5 and underline it in your Bible. If you or your wife has ever committed any act of sexual infidelity toward the other, has there been total repentance and healing for it? How does it affect the way you relate to one another now? If you or your wife have *never* committed any act of sexual immorality during your marriage, explain how you have kept yourselves from temptation. Regardless of your past, write a prayer asking God to keep you and your wife from any kind of sexual immorality in the future.

9. If you feel that your wife understands your particular need for sexual intimacy, write a prayer thanking God that you and your wife are able to satisfy one another's sexual needs. If you feel your wife does not understand your need for sexual intimacy, write a prayer asking God to help your wife gain a clear understanding of this and give you the physical intimacy you need.

10. Pray the prayer on pages 136–137 of *The Power of a Praying Husband* out loud. Include specifics about how it relates to your sexual relationship with your wife.

WEEK TWELVE

Read chapter twelve, "Her Fears,"
from *The Power of a Praying Husband*

1. List any fears you know your wife has. Do you share any of those fears? Explain.

2. Ask your wife if she has any fears that she would like you to pray about for her. Did she mention any fears that you did not put on your list above or that you were not aware of until now? Explain.

3. Has your wife ever experienced, witnessed, or heard about something so frightening that it has caused her to doubt God's protection? Explain.

4. When the _____ and _____ of fear outweigh our assurance of the power and the presence of _____, we can become tormented by a spirit of _____. (See page 139, second paragraph, in *The Power of a Praying Husband*.) Do you believe your wife's sense of God's comforting presence outweighs her sense of fear? _____ Explain. Write out a prayer asking God to give your wife a strong sense of His presence in her life so that she will not be tormented by fear.

5. The opposite of fear is _____. (See page 139, third paragraph, in *The Power of a Praying Husband.*) Write out a prayer asking God to give your wife more faith to trust in Him in regard to her fears.

6. Does your wife have a weakness of the flesh or a special area of temptation she needs you to pray with her about? Explain. Ask your wife if you are not sure. Women don't always share these kinds of fears unless they're asked to do so. They tend to suffer in silence, and this can be to the enemy's advantage.

7. Read 2 Timothy 1:7 and underline it in your Bible. According to this scripture, God has *not* given us _____. God *has* given us _____ and _____ and _____. In light of this scripture, write out a prayer asking God to give your wife these three things.

8. Do you know of any deep discontent in your wife's heart? Is there any area of your wife's life where she feels hopeless? (Ask her if you don't know for sure.) Explain. Write a statement declaring that you refuse to allow the enemy to create unrest, discontent, or hopelessness in your wife's soul, both now and in the future.

9. Read Psalm 112:1 and underline it in your Bible. According to that scripture, who are we to fear? _____ _____ Write a prayer asking God to give your wife the fear of the Lord and to set her free from all other fear. Be specific.

10. Pray the prayer on pages 145–146 in *The Power of a Praying Husband* out loud. Include specifics regarding your wife's fears.

WEEK THIRTEEN

Read chapter thirteen, "Her Purpose,"
from *The Power of a Praying Husband*

1. Does your wife have a sense of what her talents and gifts are and what her purpose and call in life are? Explain. Write out a short prayer asking God to reveal that clearly to her.

2. Do *you* have a clear sense of what your wife's greatest gifts and talents are, and do you recognize a call on her life? Explain. If you don't know or aren't certain, write out a prayer asking God to reveal this to you.

3. Does your wife have any particular gift or talent that you believe she doesn't value as much as she should? Explain your answer. How could you pray about that?

4. Do you recognize any frustration and unfulfillment in your wife because she is not using her gifts for God's glory? _____ If you answered yes, write a prayer asking God to enable your wife to move forward in the gifts He has given her. If you answered no, ask God to reveal to you and your wife any gifts she is not using for His glory.

5. Is there any way your wife could better move into what God has called her to be and do? How would you like to see that happen?

6. Often when we try to move into the purposes God has for our lives, the enemy will try to put doubt and discouragement in our hearts. Do you ever see that happening to your wife? _____ Write out a prayer below asking God to protect your wife from any such onslaught of the enemy.

7. Read Psalm 20:4 and underline it in your Bible. Write out the scripture as a prayer over your wife. For example, "Lord, I pray that You will grant to (<u>wife's name</u>) according to her…" and so on.

8. Read 1 Corinthians 7:7 and 7:17 and underline them in your Bible. Do you feel you clearly understand God's call on *your* life? _____ Do you feel you are walking in the calling God has given you? _____ If you answered yes, write out a prayer asking God to give you a fresh vision of your calling and clarify it even more for you. If you answered no, write out a prayer asking God to reveal to you your gifts, talents, calling, and purpose and to enable you to move in them.

9. The call on *your* life and the call on your *wife's* life will never be in conflict. If you feel that they are, write out a prayer asking God to give you a clear vision of how these calls can work and to show you if anything is out of order. If you and your wife are already moving in your gifts compatibly, write out a prayer asking God for His continued blessing upon you both as you fulfill His call on your lives. Give specific requests about how you would like God to use you and your wife for His glory.

10. Pray the prayer on pages 155–156 in *The Power of a Praying Husband* out loud. Include specifics about your wife's purpose and calling.

Read chapter fourteen, "Her Trust,"
from *The Power of a Praying Husband*

1. Do you feel that your wife trusts you as much as you would like? _____ Is there any particular area in which your wife has indicated a lack of trust in you? _____ Explain your answers.

2. Was there an incident in your wife's past in which her trust was betrayed and which caused her to be reluctant to trust now? Explain.

3. Have you ever given your wife any reason not to trust you? _____ If you answered yes, write out a prayer asking God to heal those wounds and restore your wife's trust. If you answered no, write out a prayer asking God to keep you from ever betraying your wife's trust.

4. Read Proverbs 21:2 and underline it in your Bible. Have you ever done something or made a decision about something that you thought was right, and then found out later it was wrong? _____ Explain. How did you handle it? Did you find it easy to admit your error? Why or why not? How could you pray about that?

5. What are three important areas in which you need to be completely trustworthy as a husband? (See page 160 of *The Power of a Praying Husband*.)

    1. _____

    2. _____

    3. _____

    Have you always been trustworthy in each of those three areas? Explain.

6. Write a prayer asking God to make you 100-percent trustworthy in every area of your life.

7. Do you completely trust your wife (to be faithful to you, to be responsible with your finances, to care about your needs, and so on)? Explain. If there is an area in which you do not fully trust your wife, write a prayer asking God to make her more trustworthy and enable you to trust her completely. If you are not sure, ask God to reveal to you any area in which you do not trust your wife.

8. Read Psalm 1:1,2 and underline it in your Bible. Does your wife ever feel that you do not seek the Lord's counsel in all your decisions? _____ Does your wife ever feel that you do not seek the counsel of godly people? _____ Explain your answers. Write a prayer asking God to give you the wisdom to always make right choices and decisions.

9. Read Proverbs 9:10,11 and underline it in your Bible. In light of this scripture, what would be a good way to pray for yourself? For your wife? What will be the result of doing that? Write out such a prayer below.

10. Pray the prayer on pages 164–165 in *The Power of a Praying Husband* out loud. Include specifics about the trust between you and your wife.

WEEK FIFTEEN

Read chapter fifteen, "Her Protection,"
from *The Power of a Praying Husband*

1. Read Psalm 91:9-12 and underline it in your Bible.
   Write it below as a prayer for your wife. For example, "I
   pray that (<u>wife's name</u>) will make You, Lord, her refuge
   and her dwelling place so that no evil will befall her..."
   and so on.

2. Are you aware of any particular dangers in your wife's life (in the work she does, where she travels, where she lives, the people around her, and so on)? List those possible dangers and write out a prayer asking God's protection for her in those specific areas.

3. Read Psalm 91:3-7 and underline it in your Bible. Write this scripture below as a prayer over your wife. For example, "Lord, I pray that you will deliver (<u>wife's name</u>) from the snare of..." and so on.

4. Are there any illnesses or infirmities that run in your wife's family (heart disease, cancer, diabetes, and so on)? Write a prayer asking God to protect your wife from the diseases or disabilities that she could possibly inherit from her family. Be specific.

5. Does your wife struggle in any particular area with regard to taking care of her health? (Ask her if you aren't sure.) Write a prayer asking God to enable your wife to do what is necessary to take proper care of her body, especially with regard to any area of special concern.

6. List below any fears you or your wife have about what *could possibly* happen to either of you. Whether these concerns seem warranted or not, write out a prayer asking God to protect you and your wife from those possible dangers and give you peace.

7. Is your wife in any kind of active ministry or service to the Lord? _____ Is your wife making great strides in her walk with God? _____ Is great freedom or a breakthrough manifesting itself in your wife's life? _____ Have you recently observed what you believe could be an enemy attack upon your wife? _____ Write out a statement below declaring that in the name of Jesus you take "authority...over all the power of the enemy" (Luke 10:19) and you will not allow the enemy to prevail over your wife in any way.

8. Write a prayer below asking God to show you specifically any possible future danger to your wife and family and how to pray about it now.

9. Read Proverbs 3:21-23 and underline it in your Bible. Write this scripture as a prayer for your wife. For example, "Lord, I pray that You would give (wife's name) sound wisdom and..." and so on.

10. Pray the prayer on pages 173–174 in *The Power of a Praying Husband* out loud. Include specifics about your wife's safety.

WEEK SIXTEEN

Read chapter sixteen, "Her Desires,"
from *The Power of a Praying Husband*

1. Ask your wife what her greatest dream or the deepest desire of her heart is. Even if you don't feel it is convenient for you now, take the time to ask her. Many a marriage has been saved or enhanced by a husband doing this. Write a prayer for her below about the specifics of that dream.

2. Did what your wife expressed to be the deepest desire of her heart surprise you, or were you aware of it before you asked her? Explain.

3. Has your wife surrendered all of her dreams to the Lord? _____ (Ask her if you don't know for sure.) Write a prayer asking God to help your wife surrender all her dreams to Him so that He can fulfill the ones that are in His will and free her from those that are not.

4. Write a prayer asking God to show you what you could do to encourage your wife and help her to see her dream realized and the deepest desire of her heart fulfilled. Write down what God shows you.

5. Is there a particular interest or activity you would like your wife to share with you? Explain. Write a prayer asking God to unite you in the common sharing of that interest or activity.

6. Read Psalm 145:19 and underline it in your Bible. In light of this scripture, how could you pray for your wife?

7. Read Psalm 37:4 and underline it in your Bible. Write this scripture as a prayer for your wife. For example, "Lord, I pray that You will enable my wife to delight herself in You so..." and so on.

8. Does your wife ever feel hopeless or discouraged about her dreams and desires? _____ Have you ever felt hopeless about the dreams and desires *you* have? _____ Explain your answers. Write a prayer asking God to give you and your wife hope about your dreams and desires.

9. Read Psalm 145:16. In light of this scripture, what are the chances that you and your wife will receive what you most desire?

10. Pray the prayer on page 183 of *The Power of a Praying Husband* out loud. Include specifics about your wife's dreams and desires.

WEEK SEVENTEEN

Read chapter seventeen, "Her Work,"
from *The Power of a Praying Husband*

1. What is the nature of your wife's work, and what level of fulfillment do you believe she derives from it?

2. Proverbs 31:13 says that this woman "*willingly* works with her hands" (emphasis added). Does your wife do the work she does willingly and with a good attitude, or does she do it reluctantly and with a negative attitude? Explain.

3. Does your wife derive a sense of accomplishment from her work? _____ (Ask her if you don't know.) How could you pray for her about that?

4. Do you ever feel intimidated, threatened, jealous, or uneasy about your wife's work? _____ Does your wife ever feel that way about your work? _____ Explain. Write a prayer asking God to break any sense of competition between you and your wife.

5. Have you observed a sense of frustration or unfulfillment in your wife in regard to her work? Explain. How could you pray for her about that?

6. List ways you could encourage your wife about her work or compliment her on it. If her work is taking care of a home and family, what could you say or do to show your appreciation for the job she does?

7. Do you feel that your wife relies on the Lord to help her accomplish her work? _____ If you answered yes, write a prayer asking God to help your wife rely on Him more. If you answered no, write a prayer asking God to draw your wife closer and teach her how to depend on Him to enable her to accomplish her work successfully.

8. Read Psalm 90:17 and underline it in your Bible. Write a prayer asking God to establish the work of your wife's hands. Be specific.

9. Read Joshua 1:8 and underline it in your Bible. Write this scripture as a prayer for your wife. For example, "Lord, I pray that the book of the law will not depart from my wife's mouth and she will..." and so on.

10. Pray the prayer on page 189 of *The Power of a Praying Husband* out loud. Include specifics about your wife's work.

WEEK EIGHTEEN

Read chapter eighteen, "Her Deliverance,"
from *The Power of a Praying Husband*

1. How would you describe your wife's past before she
   married you (happy, painful, emotionally damaging,
   and so on)?

2. Regardless of whether your wife's past was happy or
   painful, she still needs to step out of it and move on
   with her life. Do you feel your wife has been able to successfully do that? Explain.

3. Read Psalm 91:14-16 and underline it in your Bible. Often if we simply keep our eyes on the Lord, have a heart for Him, and live His way, deliverance will happen. Write out this scripture as a prayer for your wife, trusting that deliverance will happen for her. For example, "Because (<u>wife's name</u>) has set her love upon the Lord..." and so on.

4. Does your wife need to forgive anyone so that she can be set free and be able to move on with her life? _____ If you answered yes, write a prayer asking God to help your wife forgive and release that person or event. If you answered no, write out a prayer asking God to bring to the surface any hidden unforgiveness in your wife so she can move into all He has for her.

5. Read Philippians 3:13,14 and underline it in your Bible. Write this scripture as a prayer for your wife. For example, "Lord, I pray that You would help (<u>wife's name</u>) to forget those things which are behind..." and so on.

6. Is there anything specifically from which your wife needs to be set free (anger, bitterness, fear, depression, hopelessness)? Ask your wife if you're not sure. Write a prayer asking God to set your wife free from anything that binds, torments, or troubles her. Be specific.

7. Read Matthew 6:13 and underline it in your Bible. In light of this scripture, what do we most need to be delivered from? _____ Read Luke 10:19 again and complete the following sentence: Jesus gives us authority over all the power of the _____. Write out a statement below declaring that, by the authority granted to you by the Lord, you are not going to allow your wife to be tormented in any way by the enemy.

8. Read Psalm 50:15 and underline it in your Bible. What do you have to do to see deliverance happen in your life? _____ Do you believe that Jesus is the Deliverer? _____ Does your wife believe that Jesus is the Deliverer? _____ According to this scripture, what happens when we are delivered?

9. Read 2 Corinthians 5:17 and underline it in your Bible. According to this scripture, what is the promise to your wife?

10. Pray the prayer on page 200 of *The Power of a Praying Husband* out loud. Include specifics related to your wife's need for deliverance, freedom, and emotional healing.

WEEK NINETEEN

Read chapter nineteen, "Her Obedience,"
from *The Power of a Praying Husband*

1. Does your wife actively pursue a closer relationship with the Lord? _____ Do you? _____ Of the two of you, which one of you is the most in need of spiritual growth to catch up with the other, or are you both at about the same level of commitment to God? Explain.

2. Does your wife have an easy or a difficult time walking in obedience to the ways of the Lord? _____ (Ask her if you don't know.) Are there areas that are more difficult for her than others? Explain. Write out a prayer asking God to enable your wife to walk in obedience to God's ways in all areas of her life.

3. Read Proverbs 18:21 and underline it in your Bible. Does your wife ever speak words she regrets? _____ (Ask her if you don't know.) Write a prayer asking God to help your wife always speak words that bring blessing and life to others.

4. Read Proverbs 29:18 and underline it in your Bible.
   When we have revelation, we see the wisdom of living
   God's way and walking in total dependence upon Him.
   Write a prayer below asking God to give your wife that
   kind of revelation.

5. Is there anything specific that the Lord is instructing
   your wife to do at this time? _____
   (The Lord requires steps of growth and faith from each
   of us all the time, so ask your wife about this if you're
   not sure.) Write a prayer asking God to enable your wife
   to obey Him in whatever specific thing He is speaking
   to her heart about right now.

6. Have you ever observed your wife doing anything that is opposed to the way God would have her live? _____ If you answered yes, write a prayer asking God to convict your wife's heart when she is walking in any area of disobedience. If you answered no, write a prayer asking God to guide your wife so she will always walk in obedience to His ways.

7. Read Mark 14:38 and underline it in your Bible. Does your wife ever struggle with the temptation to not obey God because her flesh is weak? _____ (Ask her if you are not sure.) Explain. How could you pray for your wife in light of that scripture?

8. Read Proverbs 3:1-3 and underline it in your Bible. Write this scripture out as a prayer for your wife. For example, "Lord, I pray that (wife's name) will not forget Your law, but will let her heart..." and so on.

9. Read Psalm 25:4,5 and underline it in your Bible. Write this scripture out as a prayer over your wife. For example, "Show (wife's name) Your ways, O Lord..." and so on.

10. Pray the prayer on pages 209–210 of *The Power of a Praying Husband* out loud. Include specifics about your wife's obedience to the Lord.

WEEK TWENTY

Read chapter twenty, "Her Future,"
from *The Power of a Praying Husband*

1. How does your wife view the future? Is she fearful? Hopeful? Or somewhere in between? Explain. (Ask her if you're not sure.)

2. What concerns your wife *most* about her future? Does she have concerns about the future that start with the words "What if"? (Ask her if you don't know.) Write a prayer about the specific concerns your wife has about her future.

3. Read Romans 8:28 and underline it in your Bible. Does your wife wholeheartedly believe that scripture? _____ Do you? _____ Explain below how you and your wife view that scripture when you go through tough times together.

4. Is your wife in any kind of ministry? In other words, is your wife serving the Lord by teaching, touching, or speaking into the lives and hearts of other people in some way? _____ If you answered yes, your wife is in serious need of your covering because the enemy has targeted her for destruction. Write a detailed prayer of protection over your wife and everything she does for the Lord, so that the enemy will know he cannot succeed with his plans. If you answered no, write out a prayer asking God to show you the ways your wife touches others for His glory.

5. Are *you* in ministry? _____ Have you observed any pattern of attack from the enemy on your wife in an effort to try and distract or destroy *you?* Explain.

6. Read James 1:5 and underline it in your Bible. If we need wisdom to move successfully into the future God has for us, how are we to get it? _____
Write a prayer below asking God to give your wife wisdom, discernment, and understanding.

7. Does your wife have a vision for the future? _____ Even though she may not know specifics about her future, does she have a sense of direction for it and feel good about it? _____ Explain. How could you pray for her about this?

8. Read Romans 8:18 and underline it in your Bible. Do you or your wife ever lose sight of the glory that is set before you when you are going through tough times? _____ Explain. Write this scripture as a prayer for you and your wife. For example, "Lord, I pray that (<u>wife's name</u>) and I will consider that the sufferings of this present time..." and so on.

9. Read 1 Corinthians 2:9 and Ephesians 3:20,21 and underline them in your Bible. How do these scriptures make you feel about your wife's future? About your future? About your future together?

10. Pray the prayer on pages 220–221 of *The Power of a Praying Husband* out loud. Include specifics about your wife's future.

ANSWERS TO PRAYER

What answers to prayer have you seen since you started praying for your wife? Be sure to write them down. It's important to acknowledge what God has done and praise Him for it.

OTHER BOOKS
BY STORMIE OMARTIAN